"In his collection *Heron Spirit*, Ken Gierke invites us to walk with him and immerse ourselves in nature. His gentle poems, with their keen observation of details and strong sense of place, let us share quiet moments on forest paths and on the river. Attuned to the wonders of creation, Gierke unabashedly speaks of "the beauty of leaves, of water, and of sky." A deep peace permeates this book, and the poems have a meditative quality as they ponder what traces we leave in the world."

-Agnes Vojta, author of *A Coracle for Dreams*

"Regarding *Heron Spirit*, by Ken Gierke, one may get an impression of walking alongside him or sharing the kayak that he paddles down the Osage or Niagara rivers. Gierke's numerous meditations on nature and relationships, the river in particular, having lived near Niagara Falls for much of his life, merges heartfelt experience into poetry. His poems are personal and honest as he allows the feelings and thoughts of his surroundings to find their way into phrases that subtly recall Asian haiku and tanka poetry. He honors the memories of his parents and creates new memories playing with his grandchildren. These poems should be read slowly and allowed to settle in. They are positive and well-intended, eschewing negativity and avoiding the political drama of today's news to once again bring up subjects like truth and beauty into focus. Heron Spirit should have a place in your library and be enjoyed, time and again."

-Ron Schira, art critic

"Ken Gierke's new poetry collection, *Heron Spirit,* is a conversation with the natural world. The poems take us from playing in leaves to lines that paddle in unison with the waves of metaphors, the lines that stretch into the endless horizon of an endless river. Nature holds bold, tall titans, sentinel eagles, and a graceful heron that transforms into the Maid of the Mist. Gierke's poems observe and reflect "in true silence". Maneuvering in the waters teaches us how to solve problems and gain new perspectives. The poems fill the silence not just between each paddle but between bird calls. That is, the poems breathe with the flow of the river and bird songs. Through stunning imagery and use of meter, Gierke shows us that the forces of nature are the true constant for our future generations and "beckon us all" to enter the sacred realm of the heron spirit."

> -Barbara Harris Leonhard, Author, *Three-Penny Memories: A Poetic Memoir* (EIF-Experiments in Fiction, 2022)

"In *Heron Spirit*, an Ars Poetica and celebration of nature, Ken Gierke, paddle in hand, navigates his kayak through "the silence that white noise breeds," searching for "what is to come / downstream…" Throughout the book he acknowledges his personal insignificance in both the world of the heron and that of the word, illuminating in spare but precise language the mysteries and wonders found in poetry and nature. Gierke leads the reader to epiphanies and, yes, more questions, some of which may not easily be answered. In the poem "In Stillness," he asks "Where else would I want to be / than here, on quiet water?" An avid reader and fan, I reply "Here, with *Heron Spirit* in hand.""

> -Robert Okaji, author of *Buddha's Not Talking*

Heron Spirit

Poems by Ken Gierke

Spartan
Press

Spartan Press

Kansas City, Missouri

Spartan
Press

Copyright © Ken Gierke, 2024

First Edition: 1 3 5 7 9 10 8 6 4 2

ISBN: 978-1-958182-65-9

LCCN: 2024934659

Cover image: Ken Gierke

Title page image: Ken Gierke

Author photo: Bonnie Close

Acknowledgments

Special thanks go to the editors of the following publications where these poems first appeared:

Poetry Breakfast: "Embers to Stars," and "Fresh Air Walk During a Pandemic," *Silver Birch Press:* "How to Paddle Upstream," *Origami Poems Project:* "Endless Beauty," "From a Meadow," "Quench This Thirst," "mindfulness," "Cazadero Remembered," "Crossing Rivers," *MasticadoresUSA*: "Forbidden Fruit," *Chewers Masticadores*: "Last Light," *Gasconade Review:* "Downstream," *Well Versed* / Columbia Writers Guild: "Heron Tableau," "Alleged Contentment," "Beyond These Waters," *Vita Brevis Press*: "Water Lilies," "Leave No Trace," *"Ardea Herodias,"* *Ekphrastic Review:* "Autumn Leaves, After a Rain," *Literary Revelations Journal*: "On the Cusp," "In Stillness," *Reflections & Revelations*, edited by Susi Bocks: "Beneath the Waves," "Path to Winter," *The Sound of Brilliance*, edited by Susi Bocks: "the path of water," *The Short of It*, edited by Susi Bocks: "Passing Madness"

Additional thanks go to Jason Ryberg, John Dorsey, and the Osage Arts Community for all they do in supporting both local and traveling poets.

"The Land" is the Cazadero Nature and Art Conservancy in Cazadero, California, which is under the stewardship of Margaret Fabrizio.

Table of Contents

senses awaken
peace in the ways of nature
walk this way with me

This collection is dedicated to Bonnie Close
and to the memory of David Allshouse.

Follow the Roots

In a forest of green,
no leaves grace
the branches of a mighty oak
long past its prime.

Time and the elements
have taken their toll,
yet its majesty can be traced
along every one of its limbs.

Witness to hundreds of years
of mankind's history, its life
is seen in every branch,
each with a tale of its own.

I wonder at its thoughts,
once formed as each new bud
opened, transitioned,
and fell to nourish its roots.

My thoughts follow the poetry
of leaves as they fall
to the page, hoping to capture
words to outlast that oak.

A Rake Left Behind for Better Things

Elbows grasped tightly about my ears.
Little fingers clutching my hair
for the anchor it affords.
Cheek pressed against the top
of my head for stability.
Eyes tearing from his seemingly endless laugh,
punctuated only by shrieks of delight
as I hold his shins firmly around my neck,
dodging and weaving our way across the yard,
racing the dog jumping at my legs,
his bark the laugh that first propelled us
on the adventure that would end
with the three of us wrestling and hugging
in the dry leaves of a crisp autumn day.

Beneath the Waves

Nearly whispering, I say,
"Every wave that ever passed over
this shell is held inside for you to hear."

Eyes wide, you ask, "When I get bigger,
can I dive with you and hear the shells in the water?"
And so your thirst for knowledge was born.

Yours is now a world of numbers,
but you have known wizards and knights,
poetry and prose, music and art.

And, from time to time,
you can still hear the waves
washing over that shell.

in the moment

on the leading edge
of a gentle wave

ripples
            cresting
                        outward
            each distinct ripple
approaches reconciliation

those past
now resolved

those ahead
of concern
but secondary to
now

this wave
this moment
now in focus

The River Meets My Needs

Drifting slowly past me,
a leaf goes where the current leads.
As my paddle meets the water,
the water meets my needs.

I come to the river
to experience, discover.
The water meets my needs
as my paddle meets the water.

From heron on the shore
to waterfowl in bankside reeds.
As my paddle meets the water,
the water meets my needs.

New rewards await me
in every scene I encounter.
The water meets my needs
As my paddle meets the water.

Endless Beauty

Trees have fallen into the stream
A resting place where turtles teem
Ignoring all, or so it seems
No time to dream, no time to dream!

Kingfisher flies from tree to tree
Always heading away from me
Dives in the water suddenly
No fish can flee, no fish can flee!

Heron that stands so tall and free
Watches the water patiently
For glints of silver it may see
Strikes suddenly, strikes suddenly

With beauty that I can't ignore
Appears a sight not seen before
An otter swims so quick and sure
From shore to shore, from shore to shore

The beauty never seems to end
Along the stream, around the bends
No matter where the river wends
It never ends, it never ends

From a Meadow

edged with bay trees
madrones and mighty oaks.
Into the heart of the redwoods,

past stone outcroppings
covered in moss, on a carpet
of age-old needles.

Listen.

Who would speak above a whisper,
when The Land whispers
in a voice heard by poets?

Cazadero, that expansive house
of nature. Each meadow or glade
a room. The air of redwood

and fir a cathedral of contemplation.
Who could pass through here
and not become a poet?

Immersion

regarding Jupiter
his piercing stare challenging those
struggling for his attention
in the ebony enveloping them
enveloping me in warmth and
thoughts of The Land

madrone
random in direction
the beauty of purpose
a welcoming arc in their form

relationship
and a bond of choice
oak embracing granite
each rapt
oblivious to their surroundings

Spanish moss gracing decay
on the edge of a forest
of life and decay
defining time and serenity

bay leaves whispering
under footfalls
announcing my arrival
to the Guardians

a sphinx awaiting
a gathering of poets
under a canopy of
towering giants

insignificance
beside
beneath those giants
wedded to a need to
share the peace
this moment provides

the grace of art
as temporal as
its surroundings
honoring
its surroundings

fallen titans
announcing to visitors
Take what you will
from this experience.
Your thoughts are fleeting.
Even in our impermanence,
we are truly permanent.

Cazadero Remembered

Late October, gazing up from
a meadow in the mountains
above a deep Sonoma valley
embraced by oak, bay,
madrone, fir, and redwood,
I relive a day spent walking
trails and witnessing art
subtly married to its environment.

Led by the hand through this sanctuary
by a friend who dedicated decades
to bring to life a concept of art
honoring its surroundings,
each turn, each rise,
brings an appreciation
for the eyes that envisioned this.

Now, at the end of the day,
with city lights miles away
and a blanket of stars overhead,
Jupiter brilliant in their midst,
the experience is magnified,
and I am humbled
by my surroundings.

Waiting for the First Leaf

low hanging branches
autumn hues
hold no answer
what is to come

downstream
drought of words
frustration
lack of direction

floating leaf
repeated in reflection
spins in my wake
going nowhere

I paddle in circles
chase inspiration
little knowing
it chases me

Falling Leaves

Slowly drifting, turning 'round
Riding on the faintest breeze
Floating past without a sound
Omen of a coming freeze

Riding on the faintest breeze
Vibrant hues of red and gold
Omen of a coming freeze
Season's passing here foretold

Vibrant hues of red and gold
Gentle, still, upon a stream
Seasons passing, here foretold
A vessel now, so it would seem

Gentle, still upon a stream
Floating past without a sound
A vessel now, so it would seem
Slowly drifting, turning 'round

last dance

freedom found
in a water dance

golden leaf of sycamore
slowly spinning

matching each move
of its mirrored partner

green shades shed
for vibrant, short-lived hues

in a frosty kiss married to
a fall grounded in water

no longer constricted
tethered in currents of air

free to dance
where the water may go

short though it is
this last dance

blue on blue

my approach hidden by
willow saplings

unsuspecting heron
stares into the blue

neck straight
stretched to strike

silver flash
smelt from water to beak

head back
fish swallowed with a shake

salmon leaps, mid-river
heron turns to watch

turns back to rocky shore
easier game

Blackbird Rising

Lens framing the rising sun,
I turn at the sound of a trill.
Red-wing clings to tall grass,
wary of my presence.

Greeted by a stunning image
in the glow of morning's light
my lens pivots to capture
the beauty of a perfect pose.

Framing and focus seem
only a matter of seconds.
Avian patience exhausted,
its wings are lost in the rising sun.

Combing for Words

A school of fish
flash as they leap
in the rays of the morning sun
cresting the lake's horizon.

Waves crash on the shore,
and Toronto, thirty miles distant,
seems to rise from the water
into a midday sky, black and brooding.

Water, sand, and gravel wash
through my fingers, and beach glass
glints like the sun's last rays
that frame the silhouettes of sails.

Hours on a rocky shore,
combing for glass
once broken, now
weathered by waves.

Filtered, like my thoughts.
At day's end,
a handful of words.
Poetry.

From Beyond

Beyond dusk,
I walk the shoreline,
camera and tripod
over my shoulder.

Beyond the horizon,
sunrays reach for a sailboat mast,
to briefly touch beach glass
in the water at my feet.

A last parting gift,
or so I think.

Glass in pocket,
I climb the slope from shore
and reach the crest
to discover the moon,
rising beyond the trees.
A true parting gift.

Last Light

A trying day pressing
close to its end,
I watch your sleep,
restless for both of us.

Eyes closed,
do you see what lies
ahead or a past
that is out of reach

but seems closer
the closer you come
to being with the one
you've held dear?

When a calm settles
over you, I leave
to find my own
beside the river.

Sun low on the horizon,
its rippled reflection
is no match for the light
that once filled your eyes.

In the sun's last light,
a cool breeze off the water
is no substitute
for a mother's caress.

Night upon us,
I return to your side
to face the inevitable,
your hand in mine.

A Maid in the Mist

Beside a stand of reeds, I stand
on the shore of the Niagara,
dawn shedding its dim light
through morning fog.
On a rock amid those cattails,
a black-crested night heron
turns its red eye towards me,
and the bird's shape transforms
until I'm faced by a maiden
in a simple gown of gray and white
that shifts like the wings
of the bird that first greeted me.
Lelawala, Maid of the Mist, speaks.

Long was I troubled by the return
of the serpent that sought to poison
my people through these waters.
Only by the will of the Thunder God
was it defeated, its great body
forming the rim of the mighty falls.
But your serpent is not mine. It is industry.

While your neighbors to the north
have long sought to maintain their shore
as a parkway, it took long decades
for your people to recognize the toll
imposed by industry. The renewed state
of that shore must be a reminder
to never again let that serpent raise its head.

I realize that the fog has thinned
in the morning light, and once again
I stare into the eyes of that heron,
which turns from me to take flight.
I wake and I'm left with a fading memory,
an early morning mist that dissipates
in a warm October sunrise as the air loses
its grasp on the river, lets it slip back
into its already cooling depths,
that air now filled with sunlight.

Crossing Rivers

beneath a March sky
bundled in my mother's arms
wrapped in the thunder
of the mighty cataract

dawn's light on the river's shore
my float beside my father's
drifts in the current, bobbing
with each nibble

sunlight diffused at depth
weightless, suspended
freedom in each breath
bubbles cradled by the current

beside those towering falls
camera in my hand
captures the light
held by the deafening roar

hikes within the gorge
below that cataract
recording water so blue
pounding, rushing
flowing to the lake
and its glass-pebbled shore

a bridge of light fading
in the night as it recedes

in my rearview mirror
the river still vivid
in memory

another river crossed
highway of the heartland
massive in its breadth
as I enter a new life

my kayak floats on the Big Muddy
and the murky waters feeding it
eagles overhead little consolation
for Niagara's blue grandeur

Rising Falls

Beside the vast and rushing waters,
Within the cascade's swirling mist
I marvel at a wondrous scene

Rising moon in amber splendor
A welcome sight this summer's eve
Beside the vast and rushing waters

Contemplating nature's wonders
Thoughts consumed by roaring thunder
Within the cascade's swirling mist

Embracing this gift of nature
This beauty before my eyes
I marvel at a wondrous scene

Muddy Waters

I do not tire of the bluffs
with their grand faces.
I pass from one to the next,
straining to see into the depths
between them shrouded
in a canopy that was bare branches
just weeks before. I came here
knowing the differences
would show. The same is true
for the similarities. Would
the summers be longer?
The winters colder? It's not
the weather so much
as the familiarity. I'm getting
there, but I still miss the blue water
and the maples. I miss the maples.

Forbidden Fruit

Nothing like the birch, its slender height
bowing with the wind, its white skin peeling,
even floating delicately, your mother stands firm,
sometimes stout, spreading her arms in a canopy
that bears you, offers your delicacy to the world.

And what a delicious fruit you are. Sweet
or tart as any temptress could be, you cling
to the branch offering you, retaining a stem
that measures the promise you hold
with each twist. Each turn brings a luster
to your skin that seduces even as you blush
at the mere touch, inviting that first kiss.
Whether soft or firm, the flavor of your flesh
does not disappoint, is relished to the very end.

Ah, but then your connection to birch sets in
as you tickle my throat, and then my ears,
until I feel an itch even stronger than that
which tempted me to know your taste,
my tongue and throat swelling, begging
for relief. I resign myself to knowing
my sensitivity means you must feel
a fire inside of you, when that heat
alters your elements while delivering
a cobbler or a pie with a richness
that satisfies my passion for you.

Birches

birches
maple, ash
on northern lakes
remain with me

leaves turning
in the breeze
with the scent
of blue waters

surrounded now
by mid-west oak
hickory, cedar, green
that starves my senses

I take you north
smile at your wonder
your delight
at beauty

wrapped in white
scrolls that tell tales
of blue waters
to stir the senses

Cascade

In the silence that white noise breeds,
its waves ripple across the expanse,
reaching eagle, stag and man.

As its message cascades forth
it carries peace, if you but hear it,
in the silence that white noise breeds.

There is no tonality in its roar.
Instead, find comfort in its strength.
Waves ripple across the expanse.

Braided tresses of sound flowing,
invoking silence from all who hear,
reaching eagle, stag and man.

Letting Go

I see it daily, that rent
along a cedar branch
torn from its roots
by a heavy snow.
Framed in a pane above
my desk, it waits for me
to give it words, erase
the ghost of a memory
of something once good,
move resolutely on
without looking back.
A cardinal frequents it,
a reminder that life goes on.

Quench This Thirst

Give me a forest trail
beneath radiant amber leaves
that dance playfully in sunlight,
past stony outcrops that speak
of history embraced in layers of time
that seeps to form rivulets of life
that feed streams great and small.

Take me to the banks of those rivers
where the forest's roots reach to the water.
Just as their thirst is quenched,
let mine be so, that I may know
the beauty of leaves, of water, and of sky.

Leafspan

Eagles soar, level
with my vantage on the bluff,
wend their way along
the Osage River as they eye
the water in search of prey.

I walk along that bluff, shelter
beneath ledges to spy those eagles,
but it's the rarity of maples
that draws me here. Their leaves,
a vibrant orange, take me back

to the shores of the Niagara,
where oak and cedar do not dull
an autumn view. But I am here,
so I seek these maples, as infrequent
as eagles above the falls.

Downstream

Paddle slices the surface,
kayak glides, my wake
the only waves visible.

Cardinal calls. Turtles bask
in morning sun. Eagle lands
in towering sycamore.

Heron recedes downstream,
it's wings stately
in their slow steady beat.

Rising. Falling.
Subject to season.
Wings and water, as one.

Always, it flows,
meandering, as life will do.
River holds all, and more.

held rapt

in a slipstream
almost a daydream
eagle overhead
on sycamore branch
watches, waits as I drift by
my gaze held high
not daring to shift
or lift my paddle
I slowly raise my lens
as the raptor drops
to the water
a perfect snatch
its catch firmly grasped
it hops to the shore
gorges itself
as my own hunger
is satisfied
camera safely stowed
I go on my way
sated, the eagle returns
to the sycamore
its hold on me
just a memory

raindrop syncopation

impromptu
underlying bass
from thunder

random wail
as a wind whistles
punctuates

tree branch sways
washboard staccato
gutter beat

overflowed
each raindrop succinct
in puddle

reflection
in syncopation
lightning arcs

Fresh Air Walk During a Pandemic

A light rain that would not touch me, was
followed by sunlight that surrounded me
from a respectful distance.

Pollen seemed deferential. Skirting
the edge of the trail with shared concern,
passing hikers offered a simple hello.

Birds treated it like any other day,
their distance a product of instinct,
mine a matter of discretion.

A fox watched warily from grass
taller than both of us, as if to acknowledge
we'd never really meet face-to-face.

Cedar branches swayed in the breeze,
flinging leftover rain droplets,
a reminder that things could be normal again.

The same but different, when different
means an awareness of droplets
and we find new ways to mask our concerns.

There and Gone

Coming, going,
the waterbirds don't leave a trace

-Dōgen Zenji

It's early morning as I paddle
on a narrow, winding river
with air still and cool beneath
trees that offer shade from
the rising August sun.

A heron on the opposite bank
takes flight, but a kildeer
lingers to dash in spurts
along the muddy shore
until the wash of my wake,

sparkling with sunlight,
sends it into flight, erasing
any tracks left behind.
A kingfisher passes
on its way downstream,

the waves of my wake
reflected in its flight. Its trill
fades to nothing, reflecting
my hope that I leave the water
without leaving a trace.

The Beat of Wings

It's 83 at mid-morning and heading higher
as I stand at the water's edge. Warmer
still in my vest, I slide into my kayak.
I feel the slightest breeze as I leave
machinery and concrete in my wake.
It's a different world on the water.

There's nothing special about this river,
just a narrow band of water lined with trees,
an occasional small bluff turning it here,
there. With slow, easy strokes I paddle
upstream and take the offered shade
along the bank as a gift as I watch
a heron take flight on sighting me.

With my paddle as wings, I follow my guide
around a bend. The sun is now at my back,
with no advantage from the trees
on the bank shading each other
but not the water I cross.

Startled by my appearance, the heron
again takes flight. It turns before me
and heads upriver, its wings offering
the breeze that cools me.
And what is that breeze, if not
a way to carry my troubles to another place,
a tonic given freely with the beat of wings?

The Silence of There and Back

As my paddle slices the water,
my kayak leaves the shore.
I head upstream, wind in my face.
Not one bird calls from the woods.
No eagles or hawks to be seen.
Not a blue heron in sight.
No kingfisher to pace me,
warn of my presence with its trill.
A lone woodpecker on a dead sycamore
the only sound on a quiet morning.
The wind now at my back,
my paddle slices the water
until my kayak reaches the shore.

Embrace the Beauty

Within the beauty
of a maple's golden crown
lies no concern for loss or thoughts
laid bare by harsh truths. Though winter
will surely come, hope never leaves us.
Spring will follow, again and again,
until we embrace the beauty
of our own bare branches.

Heron Tableau

Its surface polished
nearly silver
by weather and time,
a fallen tree
lies in the creek.

Striking a regal pose,
black crest trailing behind,
a heron stands
atop a massive limb
that rises from the trunk.

My pale attempt
at remaining motionless,
silent in the silence,
earns a studied glance
in my direction.

Gracefully, effortlessly,
defying time
with its rhythm,
the arc of its wings
leaves the branch behind.

Sailing past,
then turning away,
its gray form recedes,
graceful in motion,
leaving me in true silence.

August Dragon

wings beat, move
in a rhythm that is mystery

here, there, wondering
at the rhythm of my paddle

left, right, sunlight favored
trees and shaded waters forsaken

on the hunt, with quarry
that hovers in the summer heat

tantalizing as it alights
on the bow of my kayak

breaking from its hunt,
only to be captured by my lens

How to Paddle Upstream

Consumed with your own thoughts,
always going it alone because
that's the silence that comforts you,
there's no easy way to get back
if you start paddling downstream.

So pull yourself along the bank.
The lee side, of course.
Why start now with the risks?
Stroke left, then right, head-on
into the current, meeting snags,
obstructions, knowing you can
always turn back to the beginning
by drifting along the easy course
you've followed all along.

Or face those challenges, solve
the problems you encounter.
Who knows? Maybe you'll learn
something about life along the way,
learn to set your own course
once you rejoin the flow.

Alleged Contentment

I paddle this way and that, head up-
stream as fallen leaves float past
at a leisurely pace. I arrive
at my favorite spot on the river,
in the shade of a limestone ledge
that extends over my head.

Caving in open air with a breeze
cooled beneath my rock ceiling,
I watch turtles sun on a log
and a heron fish on the far shore.
I am one more rock in the river,
touched by the sun's reflection.

I raise my paddle and push
out of the shade, startling the heron.
Winging its way downstream,
it passes over the turtles as they splash
into the water. Paddling into the sunlight,
I turn to make my own way home.

Below

Dark as night
no light from any source.
Of course, all of that will change,
rearrange your perspective.

Give yourself a second.
When first light slowly builds,
will yourself to see.

Leave the dark behind,
find shapes and colors that abound
underground, within our Earth,
worth each moment spent there.

Where water slips from the ceiling,
healing the open space,
placing columns randomly
beneath our very feet.

Completely hidden spaces,
places grand as cathedrals in size.
Memorize the sights,
lights fading as you leave.

Beauty No Less

The light that filters through
sycamore leaves, golden
these October days, glitters
on the waves beside my boat.

A light breeze rustles
the leaves, their scent mingling
with that of nearby oaks
showing a hint of red.

As the honeyed tea
passing over my lips refreshes,
so, too, does the cool water
trailing over my fingers.

And what of those leaves, dry,
yet not, as they fall and settle
on the water? Is their beauty any less
now than in their green spring glory?

Camera Shy

kayak approaches
heron on river's edge
almost in camera range
giant wings beat
gone downriver

kayak rounds the bend
heron on fallen tree
away and gone
missed opportunities
crows laugh, again and again

Still Waters

Paddle downstream
on the Big Muddy
Don't stop this time
Follow the river with joy
Be one with its current
Let it take us, winding, on
to the heart stream of this nation
All the way to the gulf,
and out to the beyond

So my kayak speaks to me

But I turn back upstream
a hundred yards
on the Missouri
Fight the current
Return to calmer waters,
knowing I would be stranded,
had I gone any farther

I do love the current,
feeling its life,
experiencing the life
surrounding it
But I love as much
the still water,
the life embracing it

And there is a life
I would not leave behind,
given the choice

Snowy Oak

Wanting to be green
in a world trying to turn green
as a plastic bag floats past
in a cool April breeze,
a snowy oak stands lifeless
yet speaks of change,
conditions deranged,
the range of fluctuations
absurd. Have you heard?
Dropping butts on the trail,
deniers spread the word
of normal weather,
whether or not it's true.
They haven't a clue,
but you know better
as you pick up litter
on a trail by a lifeless oak.

Wild Stillness

There is no conversation to be had
between us, no common ground
that would satisfy either of us,
you standing tall on a tree
extending from the water,
fresh catch lying at your feet,
while I paddle slowly past
not thirty feet away looking
for some recognition in the eye
that follows me as your head turns,
some appreciation for sunlight
glinting from the water or the breeze
that lightly ruffles your feathers
yet soothes on this midsummer day.
Instead, you bend to retrieve your meal
and tilt your head back to shake it
down your throat as I paddle out of sight.

Winged Sentinel

A thousand feet away,
eagle watches as I approach

Now sixty feet distant as I pause
upstream from its sycamore perch

Forty feet above the water
it gazes down, curious

Camera stowed, I paddle from the bank,
drift slowly beneath its stately form

White head turns to track my progress before
it takes wing, satisfied with my intent

Water Lilies

I move beside the shore,
water creased by the bow before me,
caressed by the paddle beside me.

Startled, a heron takes flight
from a fallen tree at water's edge,
its wings a faint whisper in the silence.

Paddle still, I drift past a willow
into a floating carpet of green.
Pink and white lilies nod as they part.

I pause in the stillness,
Monet's vision spread before me.
At peace, amid peace.

Beyond These Waters

Stars open among the lilies.
Are you not blinded
by such expressionless sirens?
This is the silence of astounded souls.

Sylvia Plath, *Crossing the Water*

I look into the depths between the lilies,
beyond the darkness, to see
the light held by the stars reflected there.

There is a sheen in that light dripping
from my fingers as they trail through the water.
A light not so distant, not so silent.

Its voice calls to me, reminds me that
not every siren will lead me to further darkness,
that light can conquer shadow.

I follow that voice to a current of my own making,
away from waters that would stagnate me,
would assign me to a place not meant for me.

From the surface of these waters to the fish at my fingertips,
from the trees on the banks to the land that holds them,
there is not one thing that cannot be brought into this light.

This sign is not a valedictory.
It is a welcoming sight inviting me to be in the light,
astounded by all that I see.

the path of water

clouds part as rain slows
garden seen under new light
stepping carefully

empty tree branches
silhouetted in the mist
moon wakes as fog clears

stars bow to rainfall
leaves drink in welcome relief
hope alive in dreams

the path of water
journey of many unknowns
each drop returning

Autumn Leaves, After a Rain

Brilliant, you were,
as if light could be material.

An aura is in the eyes of the beholder.
Who is to argue, to quantify?

Does its value diminish, the sooner the setting sun?
Even in daylight, you were powerless

to delay the approaching pall.
Raindrops accumulate, unless they batter.

Both present a weight too heavy to bear.
A separation, on wings drifting down.

The earth sighs to receive you, the remnant of that aura
absorbed, shape and function meaningless.

No chrysalis here, but are you kin to the monarch,
memory a guarantee of your return, come a new season?

Leaves in the Wind

Leaves whisper among themselves,
give voice to the breeze that caresses them
as they speak of birth and the vitality
they hold for just one season.
They speak of the fall dance
that awaits them, when they dress
in festive colors, shout to the world
their exuberance even in their decline.
They move in unison, turn this way
and that, shades of green
or a shimmer of subtle translucence,
always dressed for the season
until they lose their grasp,
their final direction determined by the wind.

Rising River

The crash of calamitous
rainfall creates a beast of a river
that batters its banks.

Scoured by trees with trunks
torn from their frail grasp,
gouged beyond recognition,

and swallowed by rising water,
the shore succumbs
to a watery wasteland.

We wonder what will be left
when the waters finally recede,
the banks far from their former place.

No Mercy

Rising waters have no mercy
No wall, nor bank, will bar their way
Nature will show no clemency
So take your chances, come what may

Altered routes through rearranging
Rising waters have no mercy
Currents, channels always changing
With Nature there's no guarantee

Channels confined, that should be free
Levees banked to offer relief
Rising waters have no mercy
Instead they bring regrets and grief

Complacent minds will rue the day
Bottom homesteads pay Nature's fee
Hopes and memories washed away
Rising waters have no mercy

Ha Ha Tonka

Quarried stone is railed to a bluff,
and a man leaves a sign, a testament to
his vanity. Named a castle, it towers
above a lake, imposes on the land,
until its wealth succumbs to nature.
Flames gnaw at the inside. Nothing is left,
but stone that is not a castle.

And the land lives on,
preserved for more than one man.

Oak and walnut line the hillsides,
outliving the beams and woodwork
that once graced those ruins.
From the walls of the bluff,
a spring pours into the lake.
A heron, the true master of this realm,
fishes on the shore beneath walls
that stand as the true castle to this land.

On the Cusp

I watch from the brink
as roiling waters touch
the base of the falls,

watch the maple bend
its branches to kiss the leaves
that lie at its feet.

Wind-tumbled leaves will crest
those falls, embrace the waters
that wait below.

I breathe the mist
that hangs motionless,
await the promise of new buds.

The tree stands tall,
the precipice remains,
my life on the cusp.

mindfulness

gulls wheel overhead,
cries mingled with the sound
of waves lapping at the shore

cormorants dive,
surface downstream,
carried by the current

great blue heron raises
its head, catch grasped
firmly in its bill

soft breeze off the water
carries a mild caress,
warm day or cool

beside the river
or upon it,
my mind is at ease

Voice Well Known

I've paddled to the middle of the Niagara,
drifted along a sandy island shore
to see a green heron among watery roots
as egrets called my name from the treetops.

My thoughts echoed in each wave lapping
at my feet as I sat on the shore of Lake Ontario
sifting pebbles in search of beach glass
to the call of a red-winged blackbird.

On a quiet stream far from those blue waters,
I've watched a great horned owl watching me,
heard kingfishers and great blue herons
call to me in a voice that could be my own.

I talk to the water as if to myself,
learn from my own responses.

Reflections

A slight nudge, and I leave shore.
Or do I? Witness to each paddle stroke,
it follows on either side as my kayak
moves along the stream.

Reflections double the presence
of sycamore, oak, and maple,
casting their light in ripples
cast from my bow.

I touch the water as a floating leaf
passes, or is it the passing shore I touch?
Is it shore or water that has drawn me here?
The rippled image tells me it's both.

Kayak Moment

Afloat, out of the current,
beneath a stone outcrop

Cool ceiling frames sunlight
as swallows dart for food

Woodpecker, just as hungry,
flies to a dead hickory

Laughter of woodpecker
as swallows chitter

Both calls as welcome to my ears
as the silence they fill

Curiosity Satisfied

An eagle, bald,
along a river, narrow,
late in the season.

Not circling near the bluffs,
hundreds of feet above
my kayak in the wider river.

Coursing along this stream,
thirty feet above me,
pausing every quarter-mile.

Camera ready,
I paddle behind,
hope to get a photo.

Perched on a branch
twenty feet above,
as if waiting.

Its back to me,
it turns its head
at my approach.

One hundred feet away,
then fifty
shutter rapidly firing.

I pass beneath it,
watch it take flight,
curiosity satisfied.

Leave No Trace

There is a bottom to this valley,
even for a river as small as this.
Bluffs on either side, but never together,
so that fertile land lies to one side or another.
The ages have swept through here,
worn rock and soil, rested for a while
in those fields before moving on.

I pause within narrow confines,
of little matter to all that has passed,
yet aware of the present before me.
Fully in shade, my kayak tucked beneath
a rock overhang, I gaze into sunlight
as I watch the aerial dance of swallows,
a frenzied motion of order.

Overhead, I hear a rustle within
nests tucked into pockets in the rock.
A swallow appears, inspects my presence,
then flies out to join the feeding dance.
Turtles sun on a log and I hear
the scree of a hawk, followed by
the call of a blue jay, as if in answer.

I brush my fingers along that stone ceiling,
feel as if an integral part of this scene,
if only for a moment, then paddle
into the sunlight, leaving no trace other than
my wake and the splash of startled turtles,
knowing the marks we leave on this world
far outweigh any I've just witnessed.

Replenished

hidden sun
gray sky reflection
leaves drift by

silent birds
raindrops on water
blue heron

peaceful storm
warmth of summer rain
on river

Shifting Shroud

Morning's damp
river companion
deceptively serene
mutes, silently shifts
shapes and sounds

Light diffused
images confused
concealing, revealing
visions, real
imagined

Echoes absent
distortion in
direction, shrouded
sounds surrounding
a seeming silence

Reality returns
with rising sun
tendrils, fingers
wisps withdraw
with morning air

In Stillness

Where else would I want to be
than here, on quiet water?

The air, not so silent,
is filled with birdsong,

one chorus followed by another,
led by cardinals' call and response.

Louder and more insistent,
tufted titmice give voice.

A kingfisher passes by,
trilling out its lonely answer.

The only other sound
is the stroke of my paddle.

With stillness that holds such sounds,
where else would I want to be?

Where the River Bends

Where the river bends I trail my paddle,
where the river bends, yet lends itself to my paddle.

On trees long dead rising from the river,
turtles scatter, water spatters far from my paddle.

Heron on the shore leaps to stately flight
as my kayak nears and it hears my paddle.

I turn for home, thankful for all the gifts
beneath passing oaks, as I stroke my paddle.

A boat passes and a fisherman nods his head.
I ken, as the river bends, and raise my paddle.

Embers to Stars

On a still night, flames rise
from crackling maple into thin smoke
that wafts upward in a loose spiral,
coaxed ever higher by glowing embers
that lie in the pockets between
those slowly settling logs. We sit
in a circle, feeling the warmth
seep into us, push against
the chill pressing into our backs.

Talk of the day's events behind us,
we gaze into the sky in awed silence,
a wordless communion blessed
by a blanket of stars, those flames
now as if nothing. Even as the fire
is reduced to embers, the night's chill
has no effect, for what could rival
a brilliance that inspires the imagination,
kindles wonder that knows no bounds
as it blazes across the sky?

Moonbeam Picnic

I listen to our shadows on a night picnic,
visited by words in raining moonbeams
that bring dream-sense magic.

Giving them our real names,
I sing to the stars of my love for you
with controlled abandon.

What is our image? Poems and the body,
think of them as one, alive on the nights
you love me most, over the moon.

Lake Victoria

A mist rises in her dreams,
refusing any reflection
in the water below,
as if to defy the conflict of city
canyons on a windy shore
with lily pads on quiet waters.

The comfort of bird calls
and dragonflies on placid waters
outweighs the disquiet of city strife.
Her choice is clear. She becomes
a country mouse.

Sound Stream

Cardinal calls, flashing
red in its trill, woodpecker's
rat-a-tat-tat a counter note.
Splash of catfish tail
carries across the water.

Spring speaks to me as I sit
still against the bank,
my kayak tucked beneath
a stone ledge, taking in
the chorus that surrounds me.

Not far from town,
yet far from civilization.
Significance of my silence
an echo of my insignificance.

Pay No Mind

In the moment it reflects,
still water tells you
all you need to know.

Clouds in a November sky
appear or do not.
Suggest snow. Deny it.

Leaves are raked, but still
they fall as oaks pay no mind
to storm fronts or frozen ponds.

As you enter your winter,
know it may dictate conditions,
but it need not dictate outcome.

Passing Madness

There's a madness to it
this rush to color

From a blanket of green
to red
yellow

blazing orange

and, finally,
to brown

We are seasoned in this experience

And so we wait
for the return of green

Until, once again,
the madness of color
that marks the passing of the seasons

path to winter

golden leaves
warm light on cold day
honeyed tea

maple leaf
on path to winter
will not wait

fallen leaves
carried by river
memories

bare branches
seen in fading light
shorter days

single leaf
clinging stubbornly
winter wind

Ardea herodias

on the outside
a giant bear
lumbering and gruff
quarter to no man

inside, a heron
on one leg
feathers ruffled by the wind
feeling fragile

though gone
always present
your heron spirit
never to be forgotten

Heron Spirit

three days past solstice
waves beckon joy
vows spoken
lakeshore poetry
solemn spirit presence
shared love
past and present

great blue heron lands
watches from the shore
always in our hearts

Graceful Exit

A quick glance my way,
the only sudden movement
in this stop action scene,
and the heron's head moves
forward, its legs bending
to launch that tall frame
as wide wings spread wider
in seemingly slow motion,
rising and falling in a graceful exit.

Impermanence

Paddle paused, my kayak drifts
upstream, the mild current
offering little resistance. The wake
continues to the shore,
calmer in its own wake
until rippled reflections become
serene, the kayak still,
and the waves only a memory.

River Distancing

My kayak glides on the surface, the paddle
caressing the water in a smooth, easy rhythm,
while the sun glints off each ripple leaving the bow.

An oriole crosses the stream, is soon gone in the brush.
Woodpeckers and cardinals call out as crows
take flight. Overhead, turkey vultures circle lazily.

Sunbathing turtles ignore my presence,
until my waves reach them, their plop into the water
one small part of the harmony surrounding me.

Closer to nature is my kind of social distancing.

Flames Dance in the Night

I miss those many nights
when we would sit around
the open fire and talk about
the past day as we watched
the horizon pass from twilight
to a dark expanse that held
the glorious band of stars
that is the Milky Way.

We would wonder about those stars
even as we sat indoors
during the winter months, the heat
radiating from the wood stove
slowly seeping into our bones
after a day spent out on the snow.

But it's those nights spent
around the fire that stay
with me, memories that glow
like embers and flames
that danced as they held back
the evening chill. The sparks
rose to greet the stars
as we watched for the moon
to rise above the ridge.

Momentary Permanence

I paddle and I paddle,
each stroke offering reward.

A bass, thrashing
in a futile struggle to escape
the grasp of an eagle
that swiftly rises from a river
in a slow January crawl.

The graceful nature
of a sycamore's white lines
against a blue March sky,
as beautiful as the full green
bloom of its leaves
in the coming months.

A dragonfly, the imperceptible
breeze of its lustrous wings
welcome in August heat
as it flits from a tree branch
to the bow of my kayak
to reeds that line the shore,
never still for long, until
it reaches the gray arm
of a tree rising from the river,
pausing to let me pass.

I drive and I drive,
each trip offering reward.

Children who greet me
with open arms, engage
in long talks of events
new and not-so-new,
as if they are one.

Conversations starting up
where they left off,
leaving off where they
are bound to start
once again. And again.

A granddaughter
who will read to me
the memorized tale
in her favorite book.
One who will walk with me,
a fast crawl more her speed
when last we were together.
Both milestones
in the passing years.

Places that never grow old,
never have when I was close
and never will,
even in my absence.
The sight of maple trees
when oak and hickory
have become my norm.
The blue of rivers,
waterfalls and lakes,
now that I'm surrounded
by muddy waters.

All of this welcome to me.
Permanent bonds, even
with their temporary nature,
like golden sycamore leaves
as they drift beside me, caught
in the swirl of my paddle,
as if to remind me
they will always be with me,
even if waiting inside graceful lines
against a blue November sky.

Fair Niagara

Think not that I have forsaken you, Niagara.
These thousand miles that separate us
cannot deny that you still flow
through my veins like a lifeblood.

There can be no denying our intimacy,
one that reaches back to childhood. Mine,
bundled in my parents' arms when I first met you
at the edge of your mighty falls.

Your childhood, Niagara, lies hidden somewhere
in the mists of time. Onguiaahra, your first people
named you. They respected your nature, simple
and profound, as they lived and traveled on your waters.

The sight of salmon jumping in your gorge and
the light of a school of shiners in your clear water
take my breath away. Your warm water rising to meet
cool air of an early autumn morning does the same.

You cradled me as I swam in your depths
beside muskellunge and sturgeon,
held me afloat as I paddled your waters
in the company of herons and eagles.

Niagara, you have been my quiet companion,
the many hours I sat by your shore
marveling at your wonder and beauty,
contemplating life and the nearness of you.

I have heard the majesty of your cataracts, you
with a rainbow as a crown singing the splendors of
nature. I have seen your power and fury on display,
as you rush through a canyon that would contain you

till you broke free to flow calmly, steadily,
to complete your course, connecting one inland sea
with another. I have watched the sun set over you,
enhancing your beauty and glory.

Yet while my heart still beats for you, it has answered
the call of one most dear who now shares my heart
with you. I seek what comfort I can from the rivers
and streams of my new home, but they do not run as clear.

They do not provide the solace I find in your blue waters,
nor do they lessen this great distance between us.
Before my time has run its course,
I shall return to yours, my fair Niagara.

One True Constant

Clouds part to reveal the same orb
viewed years and miles away, its shape
crisp in the cool October night air,
as we sat beside a fire talking about his youth,
mine, and that in store for my children,
knowing its light as the one true constant
throughout, as it is now, the miles no less,
for my grandchildren as they look to the night sky.

Niagara

Even here,
I am always there

My face wet from the mist
of a rainbow cascade

Hiking in the gorge
below that same waterfall

Witness to herons
both green and blue

My kayak afloat
above memories of bubbles

left as I drifted
beside muskie and sturgeon

Pen in hand, with a sunset
over orange-tinted waves

Water of Niagara
always in my blood

Final Release

When dotage arrives,
in the winter of my years,
surround me not with four walls.

Rather, set me free,
to feel the freshest of air
flow through my very core.

Let my weary bones become one
with the simplest of forces
that beckon us all.

Ken Gierke is a transplanted Western New Yorker, moving in retirement to mid-Missouri in 2012. His poetry has appeared in numerous anthologies, and his first poetry collection, *Glass Awash*, was published by Spartan Press in 2022.

This project was made possible, in part, by generous support from the Osage Arts Community.

Osage Arts Community provides temporary time, space and support for the creation of new artistic works in a retreat format, serving creative people of all kinds — visual artists, composers, poets, fiction and nonfiction writers. Located on a 152-acre farm in an isolated rural mountainside setting in Central Missouri and bordered by ¾ of a mile of the Gasconade River, OAC provides residencies to those working alone, as well as welcoming collaborative teams, offering living space and workspace in a country environment to emerging and mid-career artists. For more information, visit us at www.osageac.org

Osage Arts Community